CO CDT-462

DEAR
DAD

Other books by Scott Matthews and Tamara Nikuradse
from Random House Value Publishing:

Dear Mom

To the Man I Love
(by Tamara)

To the Woman I Love
(by Scott)

DEAR DAD

SCOTT MATTHEWS AND
TAMARA NIKURADSE

GRAMERCY BOOKS
NEW YORK

Copyright © 1993 by Scott Matthews and Tamara Nikuradse

All rights reserved. No part of this book may be reproduced or transmitted in any form or by any means, electronic or mechanical, including photocopying and recording, or by any information storage and retrieval system, without permission in writing from the publisher.

This 2007 edition is published by Gramercy Books, an imprint of Random House Value Publishing, a division of Random House, Inc., New York.

Previously published as *Dear Dad, Thank You for Being Mine* by Scott Matthews and Tamara Nikuradse

Gramercy is a registered trademark and the colophon is a trademark of Random House, Inc.

Random House
New York • Toronto • London • Sydney • Auckland
www.randomhouse.com

Interior book design by Christine Kell.

Printed and bound in Mexico.

A catalog record for this title is available from the Library of Congress.

ISBN: 978-0-517-22990-3

10 9 8 7 6 5 4 3 2

Dedicated to all Dads who make these thank-yous possible

INTRODUCTION

During a recent move, we came across a box full of family pictures. You know the ones—pictures celebrating first potties and first steps, first dances and first dates. Pictures of bare baby bottoms on fur rugs and geeky grins found only in high school yearbooks.

With each picture the memories started to flood, and they reminded us of all the things that our parents have given to us—material and immaterial—things that we still carry with us to this day, things that made us who we are today. The pictures also reminded us of the many times that we forgot to thank our parents, especially for the little things that we had taken for granted. Deciding that it was never too late, we started compiling our thank-yous to present to our parents as long-overdue gifts. We hope they spark memories from your past that hold special meaning for you.

TAMARA & SCOTT

PS—We know that every son or daughter has some special thank-yous to say to his or her parents and that some of the thank-yous in this book may not fit your own experiences, so we left room for you to add your own thoughts at the end. Of course, please feel free to edit anything in here to make it fit your father perfectly!

Dear Dad,
Thank you . . .

*T*hank you for creating me with love.

*T*hank you for running out to find an anchovy-and-dill-pickle hot fudge sundae at one in the morning to satisfy my cravings.

*T*hank you for getting Mom and me to the delivery room safe and (almost) sound.

*T*hank you for not fainting upon hearing of my arrival.

*T*hank you for saying that my birth was the greatest day of your life.

*T*hank you for passing out bubblegum cigars when I was born.

Thank you for taking videos and pictures so I can relive the memories years later.

Thank you for studying Dr. Spock and Dr. Brazelton.

Thank you for cradling me in your arms.

Thank you for not dropping me on my head when I was little.

Thank you for hanging the bobbing clown-head mobile above my crib to amuse me while I lay on my back with nothing to do for most of that first year.

Thank you for pushing my carriage.

Thank you for not throwing me out with the bathwater.

Thank you for loving me no matter how goofy I looked.

Thank you for never forgetting to feed me.

*T*hank you for picking up my spoon or bowl twelve times per feeding.

*T*hank you for coaxing the tunnel to open by going, "Choo-choo-choo."

*T*hank you for cleaning up the mess when the choo-choo train backed up and spit all over you.

*T*hank you for conversing with me in my native language, Baby Talk, until I became bilingual and could speak Adult.

*T*hank you for saying, "Dada . . . Dada . . . Dada . . ." one zillion times until I finally caught on.

*T*hank you for shooting lots of baby pictures.

*T*hank you for changing my diapers as soon as you noticed I was soggy, instead of calling Mom.

*T*hank you for explaining the difference between "number one" and "number two."

Thank you for responding to my early-morning cries in 5.3 seconds flat.

Thank you for holding a press conference when I took my first steps.

Thank you for playing "this little piggy" with my little piggies.

Thank you for buying me my very own car seat.

Thank you for pulling the worms out of my mouth when we went fishing.

Thank you for hiding my boo-boos behind a Band-Aid.

Thank you for dead-bolting the bottom cabinets and child-proofing the electrical outlets.

Thank you for tugging my finger from my nose.

*T*hank you for trying to explain where the birdie and cheese were when the big hairy guy at the mall tried to get me to smile for a picture.

*T*hank you for reading the same Berenstain Bears book for nineteen straight nights.

*T*hank you for marking each quarter inch I grew on the door frame.

*T*hank you for keeping your cool through my terrible twos, and my thoroughly exhausting threes, and my fearsome fours, and . . .

*T*hank you for telling me once-upon-a-time stories.

*T*hank you for telling me stories about your life when you were a kid.

*T*hank you for the stern lecture when I forgot to look both ways before crossing the street.

*T*hank you for crawling on your hands and knees to show me how to escape from the house in case of a fire.

*T*hank you for jogging my memory by writing an "L" on one sneaker and an "R" on the other.

*T*hank you for escorting me into public rest rooms.

*T*hank you for my nicknames.

*T*hank you for making me sit six feet from the TV.

*T*hank you for explaining why the Coyote chased the Road Runner and how Yosemite Sam lived after being shot by a cannonball.

*T*hank you for warning me to keep my fingers away from door edges.

*T*hank you for discreetly stopping me before I asked the babysitter if I could connect the dots on her face.

*T*hank you for treating me to Walt Disney movies.

*T*hank you for teaching me to "just say no" to candy from strangers and, later, to drugs.

*T*hank you for making me wash the sludge from behind my ears and clean out the garden growing in my ears.

*T*hank you for not getting too angry when you found the melted ice pop in my jacket pocket.

*T*hank you for filling my piggy bank with your spare change and letting me stick the knife into Porky's back to retrieve a few coins in emergencies.

*T*hank you for reminding me not to start eating until Mom sat down.

*T*hank you for not swatting me when I asked you if you lived with the cavemen.

*T*hank you for helping me make all sides of the Rubik's Cube the same color.

*T*hank you for listening to me sing "The Alphabet Song" over and over again.

*T*hank you for always laughing at my jokes, no matter how bad they were.

*T*hank you for wasting electricity to keep my night-light on through the night so that the bogeyman stayed away.

*T*hank you for holding my hand when we walked down the street.

*T*hank you for not letting me know what was going on behind your locked bedroom door.

*T*hank you for telling me to mind my P's and Q's.

*T*hank you for launching a search party to find me when you lost me in the mall.

*T*hank you for finding me in the toy store.

$\mathcal{T}$hank you for buying me a toy because you felt guilty for losing me and you didn't want me to tell Mom.

$\mathcal{T}$hank you for launching another search party to find me when you lost me again in the mall.

$\mathcal{T}$hank you finding me in the candy store . . .

$\mathcal{T}$hank you for making me "go" just minutes before we left for a long car ride.

$\mathcal{T}$hank you for pulling to the side of the road when I *had* to go twenty minutes later.

$\mathcal{T}$hank you for singing "Ninety-nine Bottles of Beer on the Wall" during our road trips.

$\mathcal{T}$hank you for always answering my "Are we there yet?"

$\mathcal{T}$hank you for listening to my favorite radio station even though it gave you a headache.

Thank you for discovering books on tape for children to make those long car rides whiz by.

Thank you for giving me money to ride the mechanical horse.

Thank you for telling me "That's the way the cookie crumbles" when you caught me with my hand in the cookie jar and my body tipping precariously off a chair.

Thank you for taking me to see the clowns in the circus.

Thank you for urging me to be a leader and not a follower.

Thank you for rescuing my tongue from the frozen metal ice tray when I licked it on a double dare.

Thank you for rescuing my tongue from the frozen metal ice tray when I licked it on a triple dare.

Thank you for telling all of your friends that I was a child prodigy.

*T*hank you for saving a tabby cat from the animal shelter and allowing me to name her Dog Meat.

*T*hank you for rescuing Dog Meat before I turned the knob to the spin cycle.

*T*hank you for not giving me something to cry about despite your warnings.

*T*hank you for never dropping me off at the orphanage or selling me to the circus.

*T*hank you for never telling me to go outside and play in traffic.

*T*hank you for teaching me not to roll with the punches—especially when someone was giving me a black eye.

*T*hank you for letting me put the money in the meter and turn the knob.

*T*hank you for not letting me spend my hard-earned allowance on Sea-Monkeys, X-ray glasses, or any of the other gimmicky gadgets advertised on the back pages of my comic books.

*T*hank you for reminding me that "Hey" is for horses.

*T*hank you for grabbing the plunger when we couldn't get the frog out of the toilet.

*T*hank you for immortalizing my embarrassment with a photo of me . . . *no* . . . it's too embarrassing even to write about it!

*T*hanks a lot for showing that photo to everyone when you got the chance.

*T*hank you for trying to explain why G.I. Joe shouldn't sleep in Barbie's bed.

*T*hank you for teaching me which coins equal one dollar.

*T*hank you for not letting me stunt my growth by drinking coffee.

*T*hank you for showing me how to whistle.

*T*hank you for removing the splinter from my finger and keeping the blood loss to under a pint.

*T*hank you for stopping me before I broke the bed by playing trampoline.

*T*hank you for warning me not to tease German shepherds behind low picket fences.

*T*hank you for letting me interrupt you—occasionally—when your favorite TV shows were on.

*T*hank you for packing up pillows and blankets and taking us to the last drive-in theater in the area.

*T*hank you for creating convincing excuses when I overheard you and Mom fighting.

$\mathcal{T}$hank you for taking me shopping (and paying) for
Mom's Mother's Day and birthday gifts.

$\mathcal{T}$hank you for pretending you liked the ties that I got
you as gifts and for wearing them only on
"very special" occasions.

$\mathcal{T}$hank you for saying, "Finders keepers, losers weepers"
when I found coins in the couch that Grandpa always
sat in.

$\mathcal{T}$hank you for making pitchers of Kool-Aid on hot
summer days.

$\mathcal{T}$hank you for taking me on camping and fishing trips.

$\mathcal{T}$hank you for baiting my hook with a plump worm and
cheering when I caught a big one.

$\mathcal{T}$hank you for figuring out how to stop the leaks in the
tent when it rained.

*T*hank you for teaching me an "ancient trick" to build
the perfect campfire (lighter fluid and a match).

*T*hank you for telling me wicked scary ghost stories
around the campfire.

*T*hank you for making s'mores over our campfire by
toasting marshmallows and placing the gooey mess on a
hunk of chocolate between two graham crackers.

*T*hank you for spending your summer weekends
constructing a two-room tree fort.

*T*hank you for taking me to the ballpark for a baseball
game and buying me hot dogs, packets of peanuts,
pretzels, popcorn, ice creams, and too many Cokes
to count.

*T*hank you for introducing me to "Plop, plop, fizz, fizz."

*T*hank you for buying me a bike with a yellow banana
seat and cool streamers flowing from the handlebars.

*T*hank you for holding onto my bicycle seat and running at my side for six whole blocks the day you took off my training wheels.

*T*hank you for never jumping off the other end of the seesaw.

*T*hank you for building sand castles with me and for being a good sport when I buried you from neck to toe in the sand.

*T*hank you for bodysurfing with me.

*T*hank you for letting me sit on your shoulders when we watched parades.

*T*hank you for prying me from your leg and forcing me to attend my first day of school.

Thank you for living near school so I didn't have to walk up a twelve-mile-long hill against forty-knot winds in a raging blizzard to get to school by seven in the morning so that I could shovel coal into the belly of the school's furnace so that the classroom would be above freezing by noon—just like you had to.

Thank you for always listening to my schoolyard tall tales, too.

Thank you for being a great Papa Bear and protecting your cub by calling Mr. Dudley to tell him that his little "Milk Dud" was stealing my lunch money, and if little "Milk Dud" didn't stop, you'd come over and punch Mr. Dudley in the nose.

Thank you for practicing the Pledge of Allegiance and "The Star-Spangled Banner" with me.

Thank you for buying me new eyeglasses when I lost them.

Thank you for buying me newer eyeglasses when I lost them again.

Thank you for reassuring me when my IQ scores indicated that I wasn't a genius.

Thank you for drilling me on my spelling words.

Thank you for attending parent-teacher nights and telling me all the good things that my teachers had to say about me.

Thank you for helping me with my science projects.

Thank you for listening to me practice the scales on my musical instrument over and over and over again.

Thank you for showing me how long division worked and explaining it over a thousand times until I finally caught on.

Thank you for making me feel better when I didn't get the starring role as the mushroom in my third-grade play.

$\mathcal{T}$hank you for not snoring during my debut
performance as a pea pod.

$\mathcal{T}$hank you for applauding even when I missed my one
and only line.

$\mathcal{T}$hank you for curing my hiccups.

$\mathcal{T}$hank you for showing me that Dads do housework as
well as Moms ... when the spirit moved you.

$\mathcal{T}$hank you for making me count to ten before
I exploded.

$\mathcal{T}$hank you for cooking Oscar Mayer wieners for my
lunch when you heard me sing, "Oh, I wish I were an ..."

$\mathcal{T}$hank you for climbing the tree to free my kite after
you got it stuck.

$\mathcal{T}$hank you for telling me that a little work never
hurt anyone.

Thank you for reminding me that a cluttered room equals a cluttered mind.

Thank you for raking the leaves into a humongous pile so I could jump into it.

Thank you for dressing up like a zombie on Halloween and trying to scare my friends.

Thank you for escorting your ghoul around the neighborhood to trick-or-treat.

Thank you for taking only one out of every five candies in my Halloween bag as a "Daddy Tummy Tax."

Thank you for letting me carve a portion of the Thanksgiving turkey.

Thank you for explaining what a yam is.

Thank you for lobbing the first snowball to start the battle.

Thank you for not getting too angry when I used your favorite hat to top the head of my five-foot snowman.

Thank you for waxing my toboggan.

Thank you for teaching me to ice-skate.

Thank you for letting me ski between your legs down the "advanced" slope after I insisted I could do it all by myself.

Thank you for following my tracks into the woods and disentangling my skis from the bushes.

Thank you for having hot chocolate with marshmallows waiting for me after I came in from the cold.

Thank you for drying off my soggy and cold body.

Thank you for creating magic during the holidays.

Thank you for making sure we received the *Sears Wish Book.*

Thank you for holding me up so that I could place the star on top of the tree after we trimmed it.

Thank you for letting me light the holiday candles that made our living room glow.

Thank you for believing my fibs when you caught me peeking at the gifts.

Thank you for mailing my letters to the North Pole.

Thank you for telling me that the blinking red light flying in the sky was Rudolph's flashing red nose leading the way for Santa's sleigh.

Thank you for drinking the milk and eating the cookies that I left out for Santa.

Thank you for staying up half the night on Christmas Eve trying to translate the unreadable instructions and assemble my toys before I woke up at five in the morning and dragged you out of bed.

*T*hank you for encouraging me to share my possessions—especially all the toys I'd just received.

*T*hank you for wrapping up my puppy and placing the wiggling box under the tree.

*T*hank you for filling a bowl with my dinner, placing it on the floor, and letting me eat with my puppy.

*T*hank you for walking my puppy all the times that I forgot.

*T*hank you for eating the hard-boiled eggs that I colored for Easter.

*T*hank you for encouraging me to sleep over at my friend's house.

*T*hank you for telling me once.

*T*hank you for telling me a thousand times.

Thank you for not keeping me in your "dog house" for more than a day.

Thank you for insisting that I always buckle up in the car.

Thank you for making fresh lemonade for my sidewalk stand.

Thank you for buying five glasses of my warm lemonade and for treating all of the neighbors who passed by.

Thank you for explaining why Jaws, my goldfish, was doing the backstroke.

Thank you for scooping Jaws from the tank, saying a few kind words about him, and burying him in the porcelain sea.

Thank you for letting my puppy rest at my feet under the dinner table on tuna surprise casserole nights.

*T*hank you for taking me to McDonald's so that I could order "two all-beef patties special sauce lettuce cheese pickles onions on a sesame seed bun—bun seed sesame a on onions pickles cheese lettuce sauce special patties beef-all two."

*T*hank you for buying a dozen assorted donuts and the Sunday paper every weekend.

*T*hank you for letting me read the Sunday comics before you.

*T*hank you for making me drink a glass of pickle juice to teach me a lesson after you caught my dirty hand in the pickle jar.

*T*hank you for telling me that my cat, Dog Meat, ran away instead of what really happened with the neighbor's dog.

*T*hank you for not being a "Daddy Dearest."

Thank you for being (mostly) all bark and no bite.

Thank you for telling me, "One day you'll thank me for this." Today's the day . . . thank you for that.

Thank you for buying batteries for my toys.

Thank you for setting my watch to the correct time and teaching me how.

Thank you for asking for the time.

Thank you for buying Hostess Twinkies so that I could suck out the cream fillings.

Thank you for letting me spy on the grown-ups during the neighborhood block parties.

Thank you for letting me cry and for never telling me, "Don't be a sissy."

Thank you for seizing the Swiss Army knife when you caught me playing chicken with my friends.

*T*hank you for teaching me to care for the environment before it became the right thing to do.

*T*hank you for looking the other way when Grammy spoiled me.

*T*hank you for showing me that my infrequent spankings hurt you a lot more than me.

*T*hank you for passing through your facial hair phase—quickly.

*T*hank you for having the people at the office save their letters from foreign lands so that I could add the stamps to my collection.

*T*hank you for knowing that I never meant it when I said, "I wish I was never born!" or "I wish you weren't my father!"

*T*hank you for strapping a Styrofoam floatie on my back, taking me to a pool, and teaching me to swim.

$\mathcal{T}$hank you for being there and not pulling back your
hands when you said, "Trust me."

$\mathcal{T}$hank you for subscribing to cable TV.

$\mathcal{T}$hank you for letting me stay up late—sometimes—to
watch those funny late-night shows.

$\mathcal{T}$hank you for photocopying my club's bylaws and
initiation forms at your office.

$\mathcal{T}$hank you for not looking up my strange words in the
dictionary when we played Scrabble.

$\mathcal{T}$hank you for correcting my *gottas* and *donchas.*

$\mathcal{T}$hank you for showing me how to make do with what
I had.

$\mathcal{T}$hank you for pointing out the Big and Little Dippers
and the North Star.

*T*hank you for figuring out how to eject the book on tape from the player when it got stuck.

*T*hank you for buying me a calculator.

*T*hank you for introducing me to the dictionary, *Roget's Thesaurus,* and the encyclopedia—on- and off-line.

*T*hank you for teaching me self-reliance when I asked a question by telling me I could look it up.

*T*hank you for teaching me how to defend myself.

*T*hank you for making me wash my hands—with hot water and soap—before I touched food.

*T*hank you for making me re-wash my hands when I didn't pass the inspection.

*T*hank you for always being my friend.

*T*hank you for laughing with me.

$\mathcal{T}$hank you for wishing and wanting only the best for me.

$\mathcal{T}$hank you for reminding me that good losers are the winners and bad winners are the losers.

$\mathcal{T}$hank you for not admonishing me when I wiped my face after Aunt Gertrude splattered me with a slushy surprise kiss.

$\mathcal{T}$hank you for encouraging me to bang nails for you when you built something.

$\mathcal{T}$hank you for explaining the function of a three-quarter drill head bit as opposed to a two-bit drill head bit.

$\mathcal{T}$hank you for treating me to a large hot fudge sundae when I least expected it.

$\mathcal{T}$hank you for keeping your promises and expecting me to do the same.

*T*hank you for driving me to the ninety-nine-cent matinee on rainy Saturdays.

*T*hank you for buying me my very own pizza with my favorite toppings.

*T*hank you for finally breaking down and purchasing an iPod.

*T*hank you for showing me why discipline is important.

*T*hank you for teaching me about the birds and the bees.

*T*hank you for hiding *The Joy of Sex* where I could find it to help me fill in some of the details you left out.

*T*hank you for escorting me to a tree to demonstrate that money doesn't grow on it.

*T*hank you for figuring out how to clean my Crazy Straw after I drank chocolate milk.

Thank you for showing me how to lip-synch the words to the hymns in church.

Thank you for reassuring me that I can be whatever I want to be.

Thank you for saying, "I love you."

Thank you for looking into my eyes when we spoke and for expecting me to do the same.

Thank you for squeezing the blood out of my hand with your firm handshake and expecting me to do the same.

Thank you for opening up a savings account and for helping me make my first deposit.

Thank you for barging into the room to break up the spin-the-bottle game before it was my turn.

Thank you for helping me construct a family tree.

Thank you for playing catch with me in the backyard.

Thank you for sitting in the stands in the pouring rain
to watch me warm the bench.

Thank you for the cheers that I heard when I was on
the field.

Thank you for pinch-hitting in our front-yard Wiffle
ball games.

Thank you for nailing the sign "Growing Kids, Not
Grass" to the tree in the front yard when a neighbor
complained that our worn front lawn decreased the
neighborhood's property values.

Thank you for letting my sports schedules take
precedence over your other plans.

Thank you for sitting in the hot sun and watching the
ball go through your little ball player's legs at third base.

*T*hank you for chewing out old Mr. Tortellini when he yelled from the bleachers, "Take that bum out at third!"

*T*hank you for restraining Mom and telling old Mr. Tortellini that you don't care if I break a world record for most errors in a game, you're proud of me.

*T*hank you for not being a sports parent from hell.

*T*hank you for my first name. I've always liked it.

*T*hank you for allowing me to shadow you for a day at your office.

*T*hank you for telling me, "Ask your mother" when you didn't want to say no, thus increasing my odds for success.

*T*hank you for pulling an Emily . . . er . . . Elmer Post by instructing me—night after night—to keep my elbows off the table, to stop slurping my soup, to place my napkin in my lap, to stop slouching in my chair, and never to burp in public.

Thank you for not forcing me to eat brussels sprouts.

Thank you for always giving me your very best and expecting the same in return.

Thank you for driving me around my paper route.

Thank you for doing my paper route when I was sick.

Thank you for letting me hang out at the mall with my friends.

Thank you for my cell phone.

Thank you for warning me to never pass wind in a crowded elevator again, especially when we have another ten floors to travel.

Thank you for forcing me to deposit all of my birthday checks into a savings account so that I would have a little nest egg when I turned eighteen.

Thank you for inspiring me to follow my dreams.

Thank you for taking me with you on vacations.

Thank you for working days, and sometimes nights, to put food on the table and a roof over my head and clothes on my back.

Thank you for telling me when it was time to start using deodorant and mouthwash.

Thank you for making me fess up to my mistakes.

Thank you for admitting that you don't know the origin of the universe.

Thank you for putting up with my teenage mood swings.

Thank you for smiling through my sarcastic phase.

Thank you for tolerating me during my rock 'n roll, blast-the-stereo-and-blow-the-speaker phase.

*T*hank you for tolerating me during my hogging-the-phone phase.

*T*hank you for tolerating me during my get-rich-quick phase.

*T*hank you for understanding me during my dark-and-brooding, chip-on-my-shoulder, life's-not-fair, antiestablishment phase.

*T*hank you for not grounding me for the *entire* summer after I came home with three beers in my stomach and three more on your shag carpeting in the den.

*T*hank you for not getting too mad when the vice principal called.

*T*hank you for remembering what it was like to be a kid.

*T*hank you for letting me know how much I had hurt you when you caught me in a lie.

*T*hank you for trusting me again.

*T*hank you for not quitting on me.

*T*hank you for making sure I knew when I was testing
your limits.

*T*hank you for trying to close the generation gap.

*T*hank you for insisting on seeing my report card.

*T*hank you for rewarding my As and Bs with praise.

*T*hank you for rewarding my Cs with
"You can do better."

*T*hank you for rewarding my Ds and Fs with
"You #$%&-well better do better!"

*T*hank you for not expecting me to be perfect.

*T*hank you for debating with me at the dinner table to
help me hone that skill.

Thank you for teaching me the concept of K.I.S.S.—
Keep It Simple, Stupid.

Thank you for not calling me stupid.

Thank you for encouraging me to read about the world
news in the daily paper.

Thank you for telling me that honesty isn't the best
policy—it's the *only* policy!

Thank you for letting me have a first date before I
was married.

Thank you for not chaperoning me on my first date.

Thank you for pretending you didn't know me when I
ran into a pack of friends at the mall.

Thank you for preparing a great breakfast with plenty of
"brain food" the morning of my SATs.

*T*hank you for waiting for me to return home from school so that I could open the envelope and be the first to see my SAT scores.

*T*hank you for not being disappointed when I didn't get a perfect score on my SATs.

*T*hank you for purchasing a DVD player.

*T*hank you for taking my phone calls at work no matter how busy you were.

*T*hank you for always listening to me.

*T*hank you for giving me the benefit of the doubt.

*T*hank you for teaching me how to tip those who deserve it.

*T*hank you for shooting hoops with me until after dark.

*T*hank you for helping me get my driver's license by letting me practice with you in the car.

*T*hank you for accepting the destruction of your tires
while teaching me to parallel park.

*T*hank you for teaching me to jumpstart a car and to
change a flat tire.

*T*hank you for warning me about picking up hitchhikers.

*T*hank you for not putting me in traction when you
found that little scratch—okay, okay, dent—in your car.

*T*hank you for paying the skyrocketing
car insurance bills.

*T*hank you for making sure that I always had pocket
money for emergencies.

*T*hank you for keeping the back door open
and the front light on when I came home later
than you could stay up.

*T*hank you for helping me with my taxes on April 15th
at 11:37 P.M.

Thank you for not telling Mom about you-know-what.

Thank you for appreciating my taste in "noise" and for introducing me to your generation's "music."

Thank you for teaching me how to balance my checkbook.

Thank you for teaching me to be suspicious of the words "the check is in the mail."

Thank you for believing me when I told you that "the check is in the mail."

Thank you for loaning me money and insisting that I pay you back with interest.

Thank you for making me take responsibility for my actions.

Thank you for taking only two dozen photos as I tried to escape the house with my prom date.

Thank you for proofreading my college applications.

Thank you for wearing one of my Father's Day ties to my high school graduation.

Thank you for my special high school graduation gift.

Thank you for preparing me for college.

Thank you for packing up my room at home, transporting the boxes to college, and carrying them up five flights of stairs (in ninety-degree weather) to my dorm room—back and forth—eight times over the course of four years.

Thank you for hiding your tears and for telling me that you'd miss me.

Thank you for enrolling me in the American Automobile Association just in case.

Thank you for scrimping on the household budget for many, many years to pay my college tuition.

*T*hank you for attending Parents' Weekends and taking some of my friends out to dinner.

*T*hank you for encouraging me to seek campus jobs to earn my spending money.

*T*hank you for not forcing a college major down my throat and letting me decide for myself.

*T*hank you for insisting on seeing my college report cards.

*T*hank you for allowing me to study abroad for a semester.

*T*hank you for accepting my collect phone calls.

*T*hank you for inviting some friends who couldn't afford to travel home to spend Thanksgiving with us and making it special.

*T*hank you for allowing me to spend a summer at school to wait on tables and spend time with my friends, well, one *special* friend in particular . . . who happened to answer the phone every time you called me.

*T*hank you for not surprising me with a visit at 7:00 A.M. on a Sunday morning.

*T*hank you for letting me spread my wings to fly—even though I flew into a tree or two.

*T*hank you for helping me write my resume when it was time to leave college and confront the real world.

*T*hank you for stressing the importance of having no typos in my resume.

*T*hank you for buying me my first *real* business suit for my interviews.

*T*hank you for your help during the entire job-hunting expedition and for your serious career advice.

Thank you for telling your friends that I'd be "quite an asset" at their company.

Thank you for not nagging me to accept a job offer from a company that I didn't want to work for.

Thank you for attending my college graduation.

Thank you for wearing one of my Father's Day ties to my college graduation.

Thank you for giving me some of your furniture from the house when I got a place of my own.

Thank you for missing me so much but letting me go.

Thank you for setting me up on some blind dates but not expecting too much.

Thank you for teaching me that a penny saved is not really a penny earned after you calculate the impact of inflation and taxes.

Thank you for showing me how to boil a live crustacean.

Thank you for handing down your top-secret barbecue sauce recipe.

Thank you for encouraging me to reach for my goals.

Thank you for grounding me with a strong sense of reality.

Thank you for reminding me that few shortcuts exist in life.

Thank you for almost never lying to me—well, except for one or two little fibs that I will remember when I have kids.

Thank you for teaching me that a contract is only as good as the person signing it.

Thank you for appreciating all of me.

*T*hank you for reminding me that people can be cruel and unfair for no reason at all, but that *I* have no excuse to be cruel and unfair.

*T*hank you for telling me not to cry over spilt milk (unless the cow fell on me).

*T*hank you for my common sense.

*T*hank you for stating that it is "better to light a candle than curse the darkness..." or better yet, to pay the electricity bill on time.

*T*hank you for teaching me to give credit where credit is due.

*T*hank you for requiring me to perform "bread labor" around the house and yard when I came home to spend some time.

*T*hank you for teaching me how to build a perfect fire in the fireplace with real logs instead of sawdust logs.

*T*hank you for instilling in me a
strong sense of self-reliance.

*T*hank you for encouraging me to seek alternatives to
problems and to weigh those alternatives to find
the solutions.

*T*hank you for not trying to keep up with the Joneses.

*T*hank you for teaching me about the hazards of
fine print.

*T*hank you for believing that all people are created equal
regardless of gender, race, creed, origin, or
sexual preference.

*T*hank you for reminding me that winners never quit
and quitters never win.

*T*hank you for teaching me "to thine own self be true."

*T*hank you for always being there when I needed you.

*T*hank you for giving me a healthy dose of skepticism
when confronted with claims from advertisers
and politicians.

*T*hank you for showing me how to march to the beat of
a different drummer on a road less traveled.

*T*hank you for telling me all your best homespun clichés
(the ones I thought you had created before I read one of
those best-selling little books about life), such as . . .
Unless you paddle your own canoe, you won't move.
When life gives you lemons, make lemonade.
No pain, no strain, no gain.

*T*hank you for cultivating my sense of humor.

*T*hank you for teaching me about my roots.

*T*hank you for stressing that it is important to strive for
my goals.

*T*hank you for teaching me that life does not come with
money-back guarantees and warranties.

Thank you for reminding me not to judge
a book by its cover.

Thank you for encouraging me to live my own dreams
rather than someone else's.

Thank you for teaching me that nothing ever comes easy
and that you have to work *very hard* to realize your goals.

Thank you for sharing with me the mistakes that you
made so that I can try to avoid them.

Thank you for defining altruism, integrity, perseverance,
and loyalty by your example.

Thank you for living by the Ten Commandments.

Thank you for showing me how to thank God.

Thank you for our "family values."

Thank you for passing on to me our family's greatest
and most valuable asset . . . our reputation.

Thank you for being my hero.

Thank you for a great childhood.

Thank you for preparing me for adulthood.

Thank you for giving me the best years of your life.

Thank you for your sacrifices.

Thank you for showing me how to express my love.

Thank you for being you.

Thank you for teaching me to say thank you.

Thank you for all of the times that I failed to
say thank you.

Thank you for your love.

Thank you with all of my heart and soul.

$\mathcal{T}$hank you for being mine.

And most of all, thank you for being the best
Dad in the universe!

Special Thank-Yous Just for My Dad

$\mathcal{T}$hank you _____

$\mathcal{T}$hank you _____

$\mathcal{T}$hank you _____

$\mathcal{T}$hank you _____

$\mathcal{T}$hank you _____

$\mathcal{T}$hank you _____

$\mathcal{T}$hank you _____

$\mathcal{T}$hank you _____

About the Authors

Scott is the son of Glenn and Gail Matthews. Tamara is the daughter of Charles and Odeline Townes and Alexander Nikuradse. Visit their website at www.scott-tamara.com.

Don't Forget Mom!

Dear Mom,

Thank you for letting me run away from home and hide
under the front porch for an hour.

Thank you for walking out on the porch (pretending to
not know where I was hiding) and crying loud enough
for me to hear I was missed.

Thank you for welcoming me back home.

Thank you for never running away from home—no
matter how tempted *you* were.

ASK FOR *DEAR MOM* AT YOUR FAVORITE BOOKSELLER.